The Vegan Weed-Infused CookBook

THE VEGAN WEED-INFUSED
"BAR FOOD" COOKBOOK BY
CHEF KEY LOCKE

Helping you transcend into a PHAT VGAN'S state of mind.

— Chef Key Locke X

Hey there, amazing friends and family!

I wanted to take a moment to give a huge shout-out to all of you for your incredible support and encouragement as I launch my very first vegan-infused cookbook. You all have been there for me, cheering me on and savoring my delicious food experiments, and I couldn't be more grateful.

First and foremost, a massive thank you to my wonderful Mom and Dad for creating me and instilling in me a love for food and creativity. Your unwavering support and belief in my culinary adventures have been the driving force behind this cookbook.

I also want to give a special shout-out to my awesome brother Yani, who has been with me every step of the way in this production process. From brainstorming recipe ideas to helping out behind the scenes, your dedication and enthusiasm have been truly remarkable. Also, special thanks to Roc for ensuring it reaches production and is in hand.

Now, my dear friends and family, let's get ready to eat well and experience the incredible flavors and creativity that this cookbook has to offer! This is just the beginning of many more delicious adventures to come, as a series individually and specifically crafted for each of you. I can't wait to share them with you all!

— Chef Key Locke X 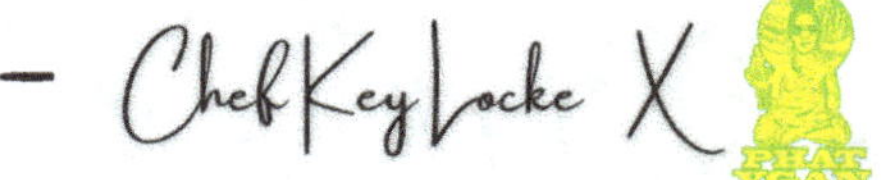

TABLE OF CONTENTS

Hello everyone!
Just a friendly reminder:
Before diving into our culinary adventure, ensure you've acquired or prepared all your infused butters, oils, tinctures, and sauces. No specific measurements for infusion are provided, and you also have the option to skip this step entirely. The potency of your food is entirely in your hands. Now, let's cook, eat, and elevate – or not!

CANNABIS-INFUSED CRISPY ONION RINGS

Ingredients:

- Onions, sliced into rings
- Flour, for dredging
- Plant-based milk (such as almond or soy milk), for batter consistency
- Cannabis-infused oil
- Spices (such as salt, pepper, and paprika) for seasoning

Instructions:

1. Prepare Batter:
   - Mix flour, spices, and plant-based milk for batter.
2. Infuse Oil and Coat:
   - Heat cannabis-infused oil. Dip onion rings in batter.
3. Fry Rings:
   - Fry battered rings until golden and crisp, around 2-3 mins each side.
4. Drain and Serve:
   - Place fried rings on paper towels to drain excess oil.
   - Season if desired and serve hot. Enjoy responsibly.

THC-INFUSED BUFFALO CAULIFLOWER BITES

Ingredients:

- **Cauliflower Bites:**
- **Cauliflower florets**
- **Batter (mix of flour, water, salt, and spices)**
- **Buffalo Sauce:**
- **Cannabis-infused hot sauce**
- **Vegan butter**

Instructions:

1. Prepare Cauliflower Bites:
   - Dip cauliflower florets in the batter mixture until fully coated.
2. Bake or Air Fry:
   - Bake or air fry the battered cauliflower until crispy and lightly browned.
3. Make Buffalo Sauce:
   - In a saucepan, melt vegan butter.
   - Add cannabis-infused hot sauce, adjusting for the desired spice level.
4. Coat Cauliflower:
   - Toss the baked cauliflower bites in the prepared THC-infused buffalo sauce until coated evenly.
5. Serve Hot:
   - Serve the THC-infused buffalo cauliflower bites immediately as a flavorful and spicy snack. Enjoy responsibly.

MELLOW MARGHERITA PIZZA WITH CANNABIS-INFUSED TOMATO SAUCE

08

Ingredients:

- **Pizza dough**
- **Cannabis-infused tomato sauce (tomato sauce, cannabis-infused oil, basil, garlic, salt)**
- **Vegan mozzarella cheese**
- **Fresh basil leaves**

Instructions:

1. Prepare Pizza:
   - Roll out pizza dough into desired shape and size.
2. Apply Cannabis-Infused Tomato Sauce:
   - Spread cannabis-infused tomato sauce evenly over the dough.
3. Add Vegan Mozzarella:
   - Sprinkle or lay vegan mozzarella over the sauced dough.
4. Garnish with Basil:
   - Place fresh basil leaves on top of the mozzarella.
5. Bake:
   - Follow pizza dough instructions for baking temperatures and times until the crust is golden and the cheese melts.
6. Slice and Serve:
   - Once baked, slice the pizza and serve the mellow Margherita delight. Enjoy responsibly.

GANJA GUACAMOLE WITH SPICED TORTILLA CHIPS

Ingredients:

- **Avocados, mashed**
- **Tomatoes, diced**
- **Onions, finely chopped**
- **Cannabis-infused oil**
- **Lime juice**
- **Spices (such as salt, pepper, and cumin)**

Instructions:

1. Prepare Guacamole:
   - Mash avocados in a bowl.
2. Chop and Mix:
   - Dice tomatoes and onions, and add to mashed avocado.
3. Add Cannabis-Infused Oil and Lime:
   - Drizzle cannabis-infused oil over the mixture.
   - Squeeze lime juice for flavor.
4. Season with Spices:
   - Sprinkle desired spices (such as salt, pepper, cumin, or chili powder).
5. Make Spiced Tortilla Chips:
   - Cut corn tortillas into wedges.
   - Bake or fry until crispy.
6. Serve Together:
   - Pair the freshly made ganja guacamole with the spiced tortilla chips for a delightful snack or appetizer. Enjoy responsibly.

POTENT PESTO PASTA

Ingredients:

- **Pasta:**
- **Vegan pasta of choice**
- **Cannabis-infused pesto:**
- **Fresh basil leaves**
- **Pine nuts**
- **Garlic**
- **Cannabis-infused oil**
- **Salt**
- **Toppings:**
- **Cherry tomatoes, halved**

Instructions:

1. **Cook Pasta:**
   - Boil the vegan pasta in salted water until al dente. Drain and set aside.
2. **Prepare Cannabis-Infused Pesto:**
   - Blend fresh basil leaves, pine nuts, garlic, cannabis-infused oil, and salt in a food processor until a smooth pesto consistency forms.
3. **Toss Pasta with Pesto:**
   - In a mixing bowl, combine the cooked pasta with the cannabis-infused pesto, coating the pasta evenly.
4. **Add Toppings:**
   - Serve the potent pesto pasta topped with halved cherry tomatoes for a burst of freshness.

13

BLISSFUL BANANA BREAD WITH WEED-INFUSED WALNUTS

Ingredients:

- **Ripe bananas, mashed**
- **Casava Flour**
- **Sugar**
- **Cannabis-infused coconut oil**
- **Chopped walnuts**
- **Baking soda**

Instructions:

1. Prepare Banana Bread Batter:
   - Combine mashed ripe bananas with flour, sugar, cannabis-infused coconut oil, chopped walnuts, and baking soda in a mixing bowl. Mix until well combined.
2. Bake:
   - Preheat oven to the specified temperature for banana bread baking.
   - Grease a loaf pan and pour in the prepared batter.
3. Bake Banana Bread:
   - Bake in the preheated oven until a toothpick inserted into the center comes out clean, usually about 50-60 minutes.
4. Cool and Slice:
   - Once baked, allow the blissful banana bread to cool in the pan for a few minutes before transferring it to a wire rack to cool completely.
   - Slice and serve the delightful banana bread with weed-infused walnuts. Enjoy responsibly.

ZEN ZUCCHINI FRITTERS

Ingredients:

- **Fritters:**
- **Zucchini, grated**
- **Chickpea flour**
- **Cannabis-infused oil**
- **Spices (such as cumin, coriander, and salt)**
- **Vegan Yogurt Dip:**
- **Vegan yogurt**
- **Fresh herbs (such as dill or parsley)**
- **Lemon juice, Salt**

Instructions:

1. Prepare Zucchini:
   - Grate zucchini using a grater and squeeze out excess moisture using a clean cloth or paper towel.
2. Mix Ingredients:
   - In a mixing bowl, combine grated zucchini with chickpea flour, a drizzle of cannabis-infused oil, and desired spices (e.g., salt, pepper, paprika, cumin).
3. Form Fritters:
   - Shape the mixture into small patties or fritters using your hands.
4. Fry or Bake:
   - Heat cannabis-infused oil in a skillet over medium heat.
   - Cook the zucchini fritters in the skillet until golden brown on each side. Alternatively, bake them in the oven until crispy.
5. Prepare Vegan Yogurt Dip:
   - prepare a vegan yogurt dip by mixing vegan yogurt with herbs, garlic, or any preferred seasonings.

INFUSED GARLIC TRUFFLE FRIES

Ingredients:

- **Golden Fries:**
- **Potatoes, cut into fries**
- **Cannabis-infused vegetable oil, for frying**
- **Garlic Truffle Topping:**
- **Truffle oil**
- **Fresh garlic, finely minced**
- **Fresh parsley, finely chopped**
- **Cannabis-infused salt, to taste**

Instructions:

1. Prep & Coat:
   - Cut potatoes and coat them in cannabis-infused oil.
2. Bake or Fry:
   - Cook until crispy and golden.
3. Make Garlic Truffle Mix:
   - Sauté garlic, add truffle oil.
4. Toss Fries:
   - Coat cooked fries in the garlic truffle mix.
5. Season & Serve Hot:
   - Add salt, optionally parsley.
   - Serve immediately as a flavorful snack or side. Enjoy responsibly. Adjust cannabis to taste.

CHILI-LIME CANNABIS-INFUSED CORN ON THE COB

Ingredients:

- **Corn on the cob**
- **Cannabis-infused butter**
- **Chili powder**
- **Lime wedges**
- **Salt**

Instructions:

1. Prepare Corn:
   - Clean and shuck the corn on the cob.
2. Infuse with Cannabis Butter/Oil:
   - Spread cannabis-infused butter or oil evenly over the corn.
3. Seasoning:
   - Sprinkle chili powder generously over the corn.
4. Add Lime Juice:
   - Squeeze lime juice evenly over the corn.
5. Grill or Cook:
   - Grill the corn on a barbecue or cook it using your preferred method until it's tender and slightly charred. Alternatively, boil or steam the corn.
6. Season and Serve:
   - Optionally, season with salt and pepper.
   - Serve the chili-lime cannabis-infused corn on the cob hot and enjoy responsibly.

BAR FAVORITES

PHAT VGAN

WEED-INFUSED VEGAN LOADED NACHOS

Ingredients:

- **Tortilla Chips: Crispy tortilla chips**
- **Weed-Infused Vegan Cheese**
- **Weed-Infused Black Beans**
- **Ganja Guacamole**
- **Cannabis-infused diced Tomatoes**
- **Cannabis-Infused Jalapeños**
- **Cannabis-Infused Vegan Sour Cream**

Instructions:

1. **Layer Chips:**
   - Arrange crispy tortilla chips on a baking sheet.
2. **Add Ingredients:**
   - Sprinkle weed-infused vegan cheese, black beans, diced tomatoes, jalapeños, and dollops of ganja guacamole over the chips.
3. **Bake:**
   - Place the loaded nachos in the oven until the cheese melts and the toppings warm.
4. **Top with Sour Cream:**
   - Once baked, add dollops of cannabis-infused vegan sour cream.
5. **Serve Hot:**
   - Serve the weed-infused vegan-loaded nachos immediately. Enjoy responsibly.

BAR FAVORITES

WEED-INFUSED SPICY JACKFRUIT TACOS

Ingredients:

- Jackfruit Filling: Canned or fresh
- Cannabis-Infused Vegan Chipotle Mayo
- Fresh Cannabis-Infused Cabbage Slaw
- Soft Cannabis-Infused Corn Tortillas

Instructions:

1. Fillings:
   - Sauté shredded jackfruit with cannabis-infused oil and spices.
   - Mix vegan mayo, chipotle peppers, lime, and cannabis-infused oil.
   - Combine cabbage, carrots, cilantro, lime, and cannabis-infused oil for slaw.
2. Assembly:
   - Fill warm corn tortillas with spicy jackfruit.
   - Top with cannabis-infused cabbage slaw and drizzle with cannabis-infused chipotle mayo.

WEED-INFUSED BBQ SEITAN RIBS

Ingredients:

- **Seitan ribs**
- **BBQ sauce**
- **Cannabis-infused oil**
- **Garlic powder**
- **Onion powder**
- **Paprika**
- **Salt**

Instructions:

1. Prep Seitan:
   - Place seitan ribs on a baking sheet/grill.
   - Season with paprika, garlic powder, onion powder.
2. Coat with Sauce:
   - Brush ribs generously with cannabis-infused BBQ sauce.
3. Cook:
   - Bake/grill until seitan heats and sauce caramelizes.
4. Serve Hot:
   - Enjoy weed-infused BBQ seitan ribs hot. Adjust cannabis amounts as desired.

CANNABIS-INFUSED COCONUT CURRY TOFU

Ingredients:

- **Firm tofu, cubed**
- **Coconut milk**
- **Cannabis-infused coconut oil**
- **Curry paste**
- **Vegetables of choice**
(such as bell peppers, carrots, and broccoli)
- **Soy sauce**
- **Brown sugar**
- **Fresh cilantro for garnish**

Instructions:

1. Prep Tofu:
   - Cut tofu into cubes or slices.
2. Sauté Tofu:
   - Sauté tofu in cannabis-infused oil until lightly browned.
3. Make Curry Base:
   - Heat more cannabis-infused oil, add curry paste/spices, and cook briefly.
4. Add Coconut Milk:
   - Pour in coconut milk, and simmer briefly.
5. Combine and Simmer:
   - Add tofu, and vegetables if desired.
   - Simmer for 10-15 minutes on low heat.
6. Serve:
   - Serve cannabis-infused coconut curry tofu over rice/noodles.

Chef Key Locke

Culinary Vegan Virtuoso

Meet **Chef Key locke**, a seasoned and innovative vegan chef renowned for crafting delectable plant-based creations that redefine culinary boundaries. Born on July 11, in the vibrant city of Culver City, California. Chef Key Locke's travels throughout her childhood immersed her into different cultures throughout California. Living in cities such as Carson, Compton, Cudahy, L.A., Montebello, "The Valley" and San Diego. Hints to her inspirations and all-time favorite cuisines are very similar to any culture's modern street foods.

Her culinary journey began in an unconventional place - a record store adorned with vinyl & lyrics. In 2013, She opened "Lyrics on Vinyl" a record store and community space named after her niece Lyric, in Pontiac, Michigan, where the fusion of music and food sparked a creative culinary venture.

This unique concept not only delighted music enthusiasts but also paved the way for Chef Key Locke's foray into the world of the culinary experience. The turning point came when Chef Key Locke was invited to host Taco Tuesdays at Menagerie Kitchen, a local hub for celebrity chef pop-ups in Pontiac, Michigan. This opportunity catapulted Chef Key Locke into the spotlight, earning a reputation as a culinary trailblazer in the vegan food scene.

The success of Lyrics on Vinyl led to the establishment of a second location, expanding Chef Key Locke's footprint in the culinary world. In the heart of Detroit, Chef Key Locke made history as one of the pioneering vegan chefs, founding Phat Vgan, a company that introduced the city to inventive vegan cuisine. With an unwavering passion for plant-based cooking, Chef Key Locke's culinary expertise quickly gained recognition, making a mark in the competitive Detroit food scene. In 2020, Chef Key Locke returned to the roots in sunny California, setting up culinary roots in San Diego and Los Angeles. Expanding the business, Chef Key Locke ventured into multiple successful enterprises.

Alongside the thriving vegan culinary venture, She has embarked on the luxury tourism industry, establishing Sol Excursions, a premium mini yacht and boat rental service. Additionally, She has introduced Hookah Mobile XO, creating unique and sophisticated experiences for enthusiasts of the water pipe tradition.

Chef Key Locke's ventures didn't stop there - enter 2DopeChefs, an infused culinary experience that marries culinary expertise with cannabis-infused delights, setting new standards in the industry. With a creative flair and a dedication to innovation, Chef Key Locke continues to inspire the culinary world, tantalizing taste buds and challenging perceptions about vegan cuisine.

As a serial entrepreneur and a visionary in the realm of food and leisure, Chef Key Locke's ventures promise not just a meal but an unforgettable experience, leaving an indelible mark on the hearts and palates of food enthusiasts across California. Join Chef Key Locke on this epicurean adventure, where passion, creativity, and expertise converge to create a dining experience like no other. Stay tuned for the grand opening of Phat Vegan SliderBar, where the future of vegan cuisine awaits your palate in San Diego CA, SMMER 2024.

The Vegan Weed-Infused CookBook

THE VEGAN WEED-INFUSED BAR FOOD COOKBOOK BY CHEF KEY LOCKE

HIGH SPIRITS & HERBACEOUS BITES" ISN'T JUST A COOKBOOK; IT'S A PASSPORT TO A WORLD WHERE CULINARY CREATIVITY MEETS HERBAL MASTERY. MAY YOUR KITCHEN BE FOREVER INFUSED WITH THE SPIRIT OF EXPLORATION, AND MAY EACH DISH YOU CREATE BE A CELEBRATION OF TASTE, AROMA, AND SHARED MOMENTS. THANK YOU FOR JOINING ME ON THIS UNFORGETTABLE JOURNEY; HERE'S TO MANY MORE HERBACEOUS ADVENTURES AND ELEVATED BITES. UNTIL WE MEET AGAIN, HAPPY COOKING AND HIGH SPIRITS!

Ensure that the cannabis-infused oil is prepared responsibly and in accordance with local laws and regulations. Enjoy your Cannabis-Infused treats responsibly!

Chef Key Locke